Notes for parents and teachers

Life-Cycle Books have been specially written and designed
to provide a simple, yet informative, series of factual
nature books for young children.
The illustrations are bright and clear, and children can
'read' the pictures while the story is read to them. However, the
text has been specially set in large type to make it easy
for children to follow or even to read for themselves.

TREE

designed and written by Althea
illustrated by Barbara McGirr

Longman

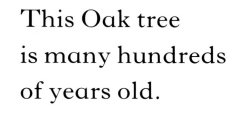

This Oak tree
is many hundreds
of years old.

It gives shelter
and is home
to lots of tiny animals.

4

Among the leaves,
the acorns rest
in their cups
waiting to ripen and
fall from the tree.

Thousands of acorns
fall each autumn.
Many are eaten by birds
and other animals.

Animals carry some
of the acorns away
and hide them in the earth
to eat later.
Some are forgotten.

A forgotten acorn splits.
Its root grows down
into the earth.

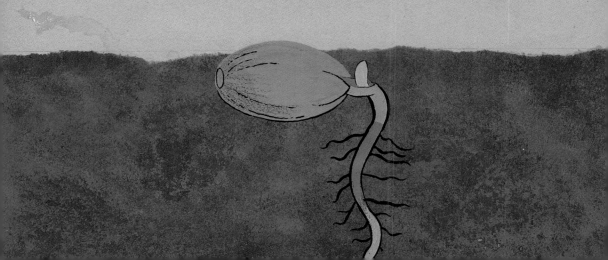

A shoot grows up.
The first pair of leaves
open in the spring.

It will grow about twelve
leaves in its first year.

When winter comes
the plant takes back
food from the leaves.
The food is stored
to help it grow next year.

It tries to keep the dead leaves
to protect the tiny buds
grown ready for next spring.

It is spring again.
Any remaining dead leaves fall.
The buds burst open
as the new leaves unfold.

Each year the young tree
will grow more leaves.
It will start to grow branches too.

Slowly, very slowly,
the tree grows
upwards and outwards.

Under the ground
the roots are spreading, too,
They collect food and water
from the soil for
the growing tree.

After many years of growing
the tree will start
to make its own acorns.

The male flowers hang downwards.
Their pollen is carried by the wind
to the female flowers
growing among the leaves.

Each pollinated female flower
will grow an acorn
protected by its cup.

In the autumn
the ripe acorns
drop from the tree.

The tree prepares for winter.
It takes back food
from the leaves
to store for next year.

The leaves change colour,
first gold and then brown.
The tree seals up the passage
to each leaf with cork.

When the tree has shut
all its doors
the leaves will fall to the ground.

They help to protect the acorns
which have not been eaten
by animals.

Next spring
new trees
will start to grow.